Rapid Debt Payoff Strategies

Crush Debt and Grow Your Savings

Written by Victoria Gunn

Rapid Debt Payoff Strategies

Crush Debt and Grow Your Savings

© Copyright 2023 Soiree Fair Literary Press - All Rights Reserved.
A subsidiary of Soiree Fair, Inc.

Legal Notice: It is not lawful to reproduce, duplicate, store in a retrieval system, or transmit any part of this document in either electronic, mechanical means, or printed format. Photocopying or recording of this publication is strictly prohibited.

The information contained in this book is strictly for educational purposes. Therefore, the author and its respective publisher make no representation or warranties concerning the accuracy, applicability, or completeness of the contents of this book. The author and publisher disclaim any warranties (express or implied) and shall, in no event, be held liable to any party for any direct, indirect, punitive, special, incidental, or other consequential damage arising directly or indirectly from any use of this material.

ISBN Number: 978-1-958287-09-5

This book is dedicated to my Mother and Father

I learned so much from them about financing, budgeting, and saving. I will forever be grateful for the tough lessons they taught me through the mistakes I made when I thought I knew it all.

I love and miss them both!

Rest In Peace (1922-2022)

Table of Contents

Contents

Introduction

We all have been there. We were finding ourselves in debt, sometimes well over our heads and bobbing to breathe under the sea of bills that needed to be paid. Whether it is from surplus and excess spending or loss of income and using our credit to pay our bills, we realize that we need a plan, that will work, and a plan we can stick to without suffering. Let me start by saying that you can do it, and with a bit of sacrifice, discipline, patience, and time, you will see the seawater of bills lowering, and soon you will be able to stand on your own feet while the rest of the bills recede to just a trickle out of the spending faucet. I have experienced this multiple times in my younger years and later learned how to recover.

It's all about the budget. You may think that is less important than paying your bills, but it is! You say you know where your money goes and you don't need it all written down to keep up with it? I issue you this challenge. Keep track of every penny you spend for an entire month, every single penny. By the end of that month, you will be shocked at what all those tiny expenses add up to. Review that list and take the total you spent on just one unnecessary item for the month, multiply it by 12 for months in a year, and multiply the result by 5 to represent 5 years. That is how much you could have saved AND drawn interest on in just five years. That is the very reason all of us need a budget. If we can get control of the small expenses that don't impact the overall scheme of our lives, we can enjoy financial success. The little things do count and will add up very quickly. Cutting what you spend on lunch from ten dollars a day to five dollars a day on every workday in a five-day workweek saves $25 a week, $100 a month, $1,200 a year, and $6,000 in five years, plus interest. You get my point. Bonus if you can get that cheaper to even $3.00 a day or less. It is the little things that can save money in your daily living. There are a lot of places to cut expenses if you look for them.

Set some specific long-term and short-term goals. There are no right or wrong answers regarding your personal goals. If it's important to you, then it's important! Suppose you want to be able to make a down payment on a house, summer home, or real estate investment, buy an exotic car, take a vacation to Bali, retirement savings, whatever. In that case, that is your goal and your reason to get a handle on your financial situation now.

As you read this book and use the workbook in the back, you will discover the easier way to pay off your debt quickly and establish savings.

Chapter 1 - When You Don't Pay Your Bills

Suppose you are finding yourself in a situation where you are struggling to pay your debt or foresee the struggle due to a job loss or other unforeseen circumstances. Now is the time to take action and be proactive about it. If you do not take action and cannot pay your bills, several potential consequences may arise depending on the type of bills and the policies of the companies or individuals you owe money to. Here are some possible outcomes:

Late fees and penalties: If you miss payment deadlines, companies charge late fees and penalties, increasing the amount you owe. These additional charges accumulate over time, making catching up on your payments harder.

Negative impact on credit scores: Late or missed payments can negatively affect your credit score. Creditors may report your late payments to credit bureaus, and this information can stay on your credit report for seven years. A lower credit score can make it more challenging to secure loans, obtain credit cards, or even rent an apartment in the future if you need to.

Disconnection of services: If you fail to pay bills for essential services like electricity, water, gas/oil heat, phone, or internet, the service providers may disconnect your services until you settle the outstanding balance. This will cause an inconvenience to your daily life and make it challenging to perform regular tasks.

Debt collection efforts: If you consistently fail to pay your bills, the companies you owe money to may hire debt collection agencies to recover the funds. Debt collections may contact you through phone calls, text messages, letters, or even personal visits, aiming to collect the debt on behalf of the original creditor. These interactions can be stressful and very invasive.

Repossession of assets: If you fail to pay on a secured debt like a vehicle or any other asset used to secure a loan, this legal process allows a lender or creditor to take back possession of the asset used for collateral. Imagine going to get into your car, and it's no longer there. The recovery process will cost you more.

Legal actions in court judgments: In some cases, creditors may take legal action against you to recover the unpaid debts. They may file a lawsuit and obtain a court judgment to collect the debt. Legal actions can result in embarrassing wage garnishment, bank account seizure, or liens on your property, depending on the laws in your jurisdiction.

Foreclosure: As a homeowner, if you cannot make your mortgage payments over time, your mortgage company can legally file for foreclosure proceedings, where they can take possession of your home. Remember, your home was used as collateral to secure that debt. Foreclosure is never a good thing; you want to avoid this at all costs. Even if your inability to pay were temporary, you would have to go through a considerable expense to negotiate arrear payments to get back on track. It will cost you so much more in the long run.

Don’t Be Afraid to Reach Out

If you cannot pay your bills, it's essential to communicate with your creditors and explain your situation. Use your words carefully, as they are a debt collector and any information obtained will be used to collect that debt. Never say that you don't have the money to pay your bills. Tell them you have had a temporary setback (job loss, illness, unexpected expense). Ask them to waive late fees and reduce interest rates. Some may be willing to work out a payment plan or offer temporary relief. Be mindful; some may close your account or reduce your credit limits. I will repeat, choose your words carefully.

Utilities in arrears: If you consistently struggle to pay utility bills, some states and utility companies may have programs to assist low-income individuals and families or those who are having temporary setbacks. Reach out to your local utility company or social service agencies to explore options for assistance.

Chapter 2 - What is a B.U.D.G.E.T

The B.U.D.G.E.T. is the ultimate financial management tool for assessing our financial needs. It is crucial to get us to our desired financial goals. When a carpenter is building a house, he refers to blueprints to ensure he includes all the rooms in the house and their proper dimensions. If he didn't, he may forget a specific room or the dimensions of the rooms in the house would be off. If he does not build up to code, the foundation may not be able to support what was built, and then suddenly, it all collapses. The same can happen with our finances; our financial health can collapse if we don't budget by our plan. Without a budget, we will drift without direction and end up on a stranded economic island without a way to return to the mainland.

If you have a spouse or a significant other, I encourage you to make this budget together. Sit down and determine your joint financial goals, both long-term and short-term. Then plan your route to get to those goals. Every journey begins with one step, and the first step to attaining your goals is to make a realistic budget that both of you can live with. A budget should never be a financial starvation diet, as that only works for a short haul. Make reasonable allocations for food, clothing, housing, utilities, and insurance, and set aside a fair amount for entertainment and the occasional luxury item. Savings should always come first before any spending. Even a small amount saved will help you reach your long-term and short-term financial goals.

Let's start by understanding what a B.U.D.G.E.T. means.

B - Balance
U - Understand
D – Determine
G – Goals
E – Evaluate
T – Track

This acronym represents a systematic approach to managing finances and creating a budget. Let's take a closer look at each step:

- **Balance:** Assess your income and expenses to balance your earnings and spending.
- **Understand:** Gain a comprehensive understanding of your financial situation, including your income sources, regular expenses, and any outstanding debts or financial commitments.

- **Determine:** Determine your financial goals and priorities, such as saving for emergencies, paying off debts, or saving for specific expenses like a vacation or a down payment on a house or car.
- **Goals:** Set specific and realistic financial goals that align with your priorities, including saving a certain amount each month, reducing unnecessary expenses, and increasing your income.
- **Evaluate:** Regularly evaluate your budget and financial progress. Review your spending habits, identify areas where you can cut back, and ensure you're on track to meet your goals.
- **Track:** Use a budgeting tool, spreadsheet, or financial software to track your income and expenses. Monitoring your economic activity will help you stay accountable and adjust as needed. Track everything in your budget. Every dollar should be accounted for at the end of that month, your balance sheet should be $0. All money that comes in is accounted for, and any overages should be put in savings so that you end your month balanced at $0.

Remember, creating and maintaining a budget is essential to managing your finances effectively and working towards your financial objectives.

Chapter 3 - Avoid Impulse Spending

One of the significant pitfalls to overcome to being successful in your quest to pay off your debt is to control your impulse spending. You have more than likely overindulged in impulse spending.

Answer these questions truthfully:

- Does your spouse or partner complain that you spend too much money?
- Are you surprised each month when your credit card bill arrives and see how much more you charged than you thought you had?
- Do you have more shoes, clothes, purses, video games, or tools than you could ever possibly wear or use?
- Do you own every new tech or kitchen gadget you come across?
- Do you replace your tech with a new one before the old one is outdated, worn out, or in need of replacement?
- Do you buy things you didn't know you wanted until you saw them on display in a store or online?
- Are you on a first-name basis with your FedEx, UPS, USPS, or Amazon delivery driver?
- Is DoorDash, Uber Eats, or your favorite food delivery spot bringing you your favorite takeout more than once per week?

If you answered "yes" to any of the above questions, you are an impulse spender and indulge in "Retail Therapy". This is not a good thing. It will prevent you from saving for important things like a house, a new car, a vacation, or retirement. You must set some financial goals and resist spending money on items that don't matter in the long run.

Impulse spending will not only put a strain on your finances but your relationships, as well. First, to overcome the problem, learn to separate your needs from your wants. Advertisers blitz us hawking their products at us 24/7. The trick is to give yourself a cooling-off period before purchasing anything that you have not planned for. When you go shopping, make a list and take only enough cash to pay for what you have planned to buy. Leave your credit cards at home. If you see something you desire, give yourself two weeks to decide if it is something you need or can easily do without. By following this simple solution, you will mend your financial fences and your relationships.

Chapter 4 - Savings Means, Paying Yourself First

Your savings should be a lifelong expense that you pay into with no exception to the rule of skipping, paying late, or not paying it all. You need to pay into your expense so that you have a personal no-fee credit to tap into when you need it for emergencies or planned purchases or events! It is often overlooked as an expense because it doesn't involve immediate consumption or tangible benefits. However, saving is crucial in securing your economic well-being and achieving long-term goals.

Here are some reasons why savings should be considered as an expense:

1. **Emergency Fund Life:**
   Life is unpredictable and unexpected expenses can arise anytime, such as medical emergencies, car repairs, or job loss. An emergency fund allows you to handle these situations without debt or disrupting your financial stability. Saving for emergencies is like paying for insurance against unexpected events.

2. **Future Goals Saving:**
   It allows you to work towards your future goals, whether buying a house, starting a business, funding education, or retiring comfortably. By consistently setting aside money as an expense, you are investing in your future and creating opportunities for personal and financial growth.

3. **Retirement Planning:**
   Saving for retirement is crucial to ensure financial independence and a comfortable lifestyle in your golden years. Treating retirement savings as an expense, you prioritize building a nest egg for the future. Contributions to retirement accounts, such as a 401(k) or an individual retirement account (IRA), can benefit from compounding over time, allowing your savings to grow significantly.

4. **Financial Security:**
   Saving as an expense provides a safety net and financial security. It helps you cope with unforeseen circumstances, reduces financial stress, and provides peace of mind. Having savings cushions you against unexpected setbacks and gives you more control over your financial situation.

5. **Capital for Investments:**
   Saving money also enables you to explore investment opportunities, whether investing in stock real estate or starting a business. Having capital available allows you to take advantage of potentially profitable ventures. Treating savings as an expense helps you allocate funds for these investment opportunities.

6. **Debt Management:**

   Saving can help you avoid or reduce debt. By consistently saving, you build a financial buffer that can be used to cover expenses instead of relying on credit cards or loans. This approach can reduce interest payments, improve your credit score, and lead to better overall financial health.

7. **Flexibility and Freedom:**

   Saving money provides you with flexibility and freedom in making life choices. It allows you to pursue new opportunities, take career risks, travel, or even take time off work without financial stress. Treating savings as an expense ensures you prioritize building the financial freedom necessary to make such choices.

Saving should be treated as an expense because it is essential to a healthy financial plan. By prioritizing saving, you establish a solid financial foundation, protect yourself against emergencies, work towards future goals, and gain financial security and independence.

Chapter 5 - 8 Steps to Create Your Financial Blueprint

I have outlined below 8 steps to take to create your financial blueprint. Utilizing this strategy will allow you to see the big picture and put actionable steps in place to get your debts paid faster. These simple debt reduction techniques include budgeting techniques and quick money management advice to jump start your savings. Just remember that before you begin making payments, make a list of every debt you have. You will need this to include everything.

1. Make a list of all your debt.
2. Create a budget.
3. Apply Debt Avalanche.
4. Apply Debt Snowball.
5. Pay more than the minimum balance.
6. Take advantage of balance transfers.
7. Stop your credit card spending and or cash advances.
8. Avoid returning to bad habits when you reach your goal.

1. **Make a list of all your debt.**

   When you list all your debt, include its name, type, balance due, and interest rate. Determine whether this debt is a fixed or variable expense. If it is the same amount every month, then it is a fixed expense. If it fluctuates like a utility bill or it's an expense that is not monthly but shows up, then it is a variable expense. You can use the debt building sheet in the back of this workbook as a guide.

2. **Create a budget**

   Start by tracking your income and expenses with a monthly budget to repay your debt. Review all your income sources, salaries, other jobs, dividend payments, rebates, refunds, etc., and any source that will bring money into your account. Notate if this is a monthly, quarterly, or even an ad hoc type of income that comes once in a while. You can use something as simple as a spreadsheet or more complex, utilizing budgeting apps that track every expense and debt payment. Search online for those apps that may meet your goals. I have also included a budget worksheet in the back of this book to get you started.

3. **Apply Debt Avalanche**

   This strategy is used when you first tackle the most expensive debt with the highest interest rates. During this repayment strategy, you should continue paying the minimum on your other, less costly debts but focus any extra cash available on the most expensive debts. I highly recommend this on debt with interest rates of 18%-35%+. As you pay down these debts, you will save money on the interest rate on the debt. Mathematically speaking, this is a sound approach for some accounts that took pure advantage of you with that insane interest. Sadly, it happens, but it is not your fault. This strategy will save you money in the long run by getting rid of these bad debts, like credit card debt, faster.

4. **Apply Debt Snowball**

   Unlike Step 3 in the Debt Avalanche, the Debt Snowball is the opposite. Here is where you pay the smallest debts and work your way up. Think of a debt you owe with $200 or $300 to pay it off. You could pay that off in one or two payments and curb that card or debt for a while. The psychology behind this is that you will feel the instant victory of conquering the "low-hanging fruit," and it will motivate you to continue to do the same for the next one and so on. The discipline here is only to use that card again if it fits your budget. Until you control over 70% or more of your budget, I would not think of using it for a while. Enjoy the achievement.

5. **Pay more than the minimum balance**

   Each debt has a minimum balance they expect you to pay monthly. A trick here is that if your credit card is up to its limit, paying the minimum will not cover the interest they charge, which can bring you over the limit. Some cards (hopefully not yours) will charge an over-the-limit fee and report this to the credit bureaus. To truly make any headway on your debts, you'll need to pay more than the minimum balance on your monthly credit card statements. Add up the minimum and the amount of interest you were charged last month and try to make that your monthly payment. Consider $10 or more above the minimum if that is too steep. When you pay just the minimum, it will take longer to pay off, and you are paying more in interest. Consider putting extra money toward the principal on a home mortgage or car loan so long as those additional payments wouldn't be better used on other debts. You can adjust your budget for those payments when you have more money to work with from paying down other debt.

6. **Take advantage of balance transfers**

   This is a little tricky, but it can work. If you have good credit and can get approved for a credit card with a low introductory rate, go for it. Make sure you will also be able to do a balance transfer from an existing credit card you have to the new one. Select your highest interest rate credit card to do that balance transfer. Not only will you have paid off that high-interest credit card payment, you will be saving money in interest on the new one you transferred the debt to. Monitor this payment to avoid catching up with an increasing interest after the introductory rate timeline expires. Try to pay this off before the rate increases if they have one. If the lower rate is consistent, managing debt, using credit cards, which typically come with high-interest rates, can be extremely costly. Use with extreme caution.

7. **Stop your credit card spending and or cash advances**

This topic should have been at the top of the list. However, I am mentioning it here as the first 6 steps will take some time to do and focus on. Not all debt is credit card debt, so we address it here. Overspending is quickly and easily done by using credit cards. Cash advances are easy to get from your credit cards. Both practices need to be stopped! This can add to your debt, causing a vicious cycle. The cash advances have a much higher interest rate and are only considered paid once you reach a zero balance on your statement. Therefore, they will keep charging you the higher interest on your statements. It's regarded as the last to get repaid. I encourage you to remove your credit cards from all your online store accounts to reduce the risk of impulse purchases. Consider also removing them from your wallet, only allowing 1 or 2 for extremely dire emergencies. I understand that crap can happen, and we need the backup. Just promise if an emergency arises, avoid a cash advance. Reallocate your budget to account for the crisis, and immediately get back on track. Do not let it derail you from your financial goal.

8. **Avoid returning to bad habits when you reach your goal**
   Take the time to understand how you came into debt to avoid finding yourself there again. Overspending and accumulating large debts is often a behavioral issue. Be honest about your daily habits and spending, then make the necessary lifestyle changes to repay your debts. Set your priorities straight. Ensure you cover your essential expenses like food, housing, and health. Then review all the other discretionary items. To avoid debt, decide whether it is a necessary or discretionary expense. You will be surprised by how much of that is discretionary. Once you reach your goal, you'll need to keep up your good money habits to stay debt-free and avoid the underlying reason for spending; otherwise, the debt will come right back!

Chapter 6 - Increase Your Income

To help pay off debt, you can also look at ways to increase your income or bring in extra money. Diversifying your income sources is a prudent strategy to improve your overall earnings. Relying solely on a single income stream can be risky. Fortunately, you can explore several strategies and avenues to boost your income. Let's explore various approaches and techniques to help you achieve your financial goals and enhance your income. Let's look at the best ways with little to no cost as we work to reduce our debt, not increase it.

1. **Negotiate a Raise or Promotions:**
   If you are currently employed, negotiate a raise or seek a promotion within your organization. It is an effective way to increase your income. Prepare a compelling case highlighting your accomplishments, contributions, and value to the company. Research salary benchmarks and be prepared to negotiate your terms. Remember to showcase your enthusiasm, dedication, and commitment to the organization's success.

2. **Explore side hustles and freelancing**:
   In the gig economy, numerous opportunities exist to generate extra income outside your primary job. Consider exploring side hustles or freelancing in your spare time. Identify your skills and interests and leverage platforms like freelancing websites. Use your talents and hobbies to earn additional income.

3. **Monetize Your Hobbies or Talents:**
   If you possess a particular talent or are passionate about a hobby, consider monetizing it. For instance, if you're skilled at singing, painting, or playing a musical instrument, offer music, painting, and singing lessons on the side. If you have a flare for writing, explore freelance writing opportunities or start a blog that generates revenue through advertisements or sponsored content. Look for creative ways to turn your passions into income-generating ventures. Remember, you don't have to spend money as you can attract sponsors or advertisers to pay for the incidentals you may need. Otherwise, all the rest can go towards your debt reduction and savings.

4. **Utilize the Power of the Internet:**
   The internet offers many opportunities to earn money and explore avenues like affiliate marketing content creation on platforms like YouTube or Twitch. Participate in online surveys or market research studies. Leverage social media platforms to build a personal brand or showcase your expertise which can attract new clients or business opportunities. Consider E-commerce through platforms like Etsy or Shopify. ***Note:*** Etsy and Shopify have monthly expenses associated with the account, so you must consider that in the budget. You can sell digital products that cost nothing if you make them yourself. You can setup up a drop shipping method where you only

buy a product when it is sold, and the cost is taken out of the sale. The item is shipped directly to the customer, so you don't hold any inventory and do not have to tie up any money in the process. The remainder is your profit!

5. **Enhance Your Skill and Education:**
   Investing in your education and inquiring new skills can significantly impact your earning potential. Consider pursuing additional certifications, attending workshops or seminars, or enrolling in an online course relevant to your field. Gaining expertise in staying updated with industry trends can make you more valuable to employers or clients, leading to higher pay opportunities. I suggest or recommend you consider your budget before taking this approach. Courses, workshops, and even seminars can be costly. However, there are several free alternatives that you could research first before considering dipping into a budget to cover the costs for these while you're still trying to pay off your debt.

6. **Sell, Sell, Sell:**
   Come up with some extra cash by selling unwanted items that you own. It is easier than ever with online shops specializing in consignment clothing and sites like Facebook, Craigslist, Declutter, and Ebay where just about anything can be bought and sold. Put all the money from your sales toward paying down your debts. You will make extra money and clean up the clutter you may have lying around.

By diversifying, you reduce the impact of any potential setbacks or fluctuations in one area. Consider combining a stable job with side hustles and passive income streams to build a more robust financial foundation. You will increase the speed of paying off your debt and truly enhance the amount of savings you will have in the process.

Chapter 7 - Debt Consolidation

Debt consolidation is a financial strategy combining multiple debts into a single loan or credit line. Debt consolidation aims to simplify your finances and reduce your overall interest rates, making it easier to manage and pay off your debts.

Here's how Debt Consolidation typically works.

Assessing Your Debt:
Start by evaluating your debts, including credit card balances, personal loans, medical bills, or other outstanding obligations. Take note of each debt's interest rate, minimum monthly payments, and repayment terms.

1. **Explore consolidation Options**:
   Once you have a clear understanding of your debts, you can explore various debt consolidation options. These options may include:

2. **Debt Consolidation Loan** - You can apply for a personal loan from a bank, credit union, or online lender to pay off your existing debts. The loan amount should be sufficient to cover the total outstanding balances. With a debt consolidation loan, you'll make a single monthly payment to the lender instead of multiple payments to different creditors.

3. **Home Equity Line of Credit** - If you own a home and have built up equity, you can borrow against it using a home equity loan or home equity line of credit (HELOC). These options allow you to use the equity in your home to pay off your debts. Remember that your home is issued as collateral, so there's a risk of losing it if you can't repay the loan.

4. **Applying for Consolidation** - Once you've chosen the most suitable debt consolidation option, you must apply for the loan or credit line. The lender will review your credit history, income, and other financial factors to determine if you qualify for the consolidation option and what interest rate you will receive.

5. **Paying off Existing Debt** – If your consolidation application is approved, the funds from the new loan or credit line will be used to pay off your debts. This means you'll no longer owe money to multiple creditors but will have a single debt to repay. Your single monthly payment aims to make this debt more manageable and potentially reduce your interest rate, which can save you money over time.

Debt Consolidation can be a helpful tool for simplifying your financial situation and potentially reducing your interest costs. Considering the terms and charges associated with consolidation options is essential before deciding. It's also crucial to address any underlining issues that led to your debt accumulation, such as overspending or poor budgeting, to avoid falling back into debt in the future. Just because you paid it off doesn't mean you should use it. Debt repayment can be overwhelming; this is another option if your debt is out of control.

Chapter 8 - Debt Counseling

It may be time to consider Debt Counseling. Debt Counseling may be your best option if you cannot take steps to get it under control yourself or do not qualify for a debt consolidation plan. Debt Counseling, or credit or financial counseling, is designed to assist individuals facing financial difficulties and struggling with debt management. Debt counseling aims to provide guidance, education, and support to help individuals regain control of their finances and improve their overall financial well-being.

Here are the key aspects of Debt Counseling:

Financial Assessment - During debt counseling, a certified credit counselor or financial expert will evaluate your financial situation by analyzing your income, expenses, assets, and debts. This assessment helps them understand the extent of your financial difficulties and develop a personalized plan.

Budgeting and Money Management - Debt counselors work with individuals to create a realistic budget based on their income and expenses. They help prioritize costs, identify areas for cost-cutting, and develop strategies for managing money effectively. The goal is to help individuals gain control over their spending habits and create a sustainable financial plan.

Debt Repayment Strategies - Debt counselors assist individuals with developing a debt repayment strategy tailored to their specific circumstances. They may negotiate with creditors on behalf of the individual to reduce interest rates, waive fees, or establish more favorable repayment terms. Counselors may also suggest debt consolidation options or debt management plans to simplify repayments.

Financial Education - Debt counselors provide valuable financial education to clients. Counselors explain credit scores, interest rates, and debt-income ratios. This helps individuals better understand a financial situation and make informed decisions. They also guide building good financial habits managing credit responsibly, and avoiding future debt problems.

Support and Guidance - Debt counselors offer ongoing support throughout the debt repayment. They serve as a resource for clients, answering questions, providing advice, and offering encouragement. They help individuals stay motivated and focused on their financial goals, ensuring they progress in reducing their debt burden.
It's important to note that debt counseling is typically provided by nonprofit organizations. Credit counseling agencies or government approved agencies often charge nominal fees or offer free counseling services depending on the individual's financial situation. Debt counseling can be a valuable resource for individuals struggling with debt. It provides expert

guidance, practical tools, and emotional support to help them regain financial stability and work towards a debt-free future.

Chapter 9 - Bankruptcy

When all else fails, there is always bankruptcy. This strategy should be avoided as you lose your credit power and must rebuild. If time is your friend, then this could be a strategy that is best for you. Bankruptcy is a legal process designed to relieve individuals who cannot repay their debts. It is a formal declaration that an individual cannot meet their financial obligation and seeks protection from creditors. When someone files for bankruptcy, it is because their debts have become overwhelming, and they cannot make payments as agreed upon. Bankruptcy allows the debtor to eliminate or restructure their debts and obtain a fresh financial start.

Bankruptcy proceedings are overseen by a bankruptcy court, which evaluates the debtor's financial situation, assets, liabilities, and income to determine the most appropriate course of action. The Court may appoint a trustee to administer the bankruptcy process and ensure that the debt complies with the applicable laws and regulations. There are different types of bankruptcies, but the most common forms are Chapter 7 and Chapter 13 for individuals. Chapter 11 is used for business.

Chapter 7 - eligible debts are typically discharged, meaning they are eliminated, allowing the individual to start anew. However, not all debts, such as certain taxes, child support, and student loans, can be discharged.

Chapter 13 - allows individuals with a steady income to create a repayment plan to pay off their debts over a time period of 3 to 5 years. This enables individuals to keep their assets while repaying their creditors according to the court-approved plan. Chapter 13 is best used for the debts that cannot be discharged through Chapter 7, or it can potentially save your home from foreclosure if you need the time to get caught up on the arrears.

Chapter 11 - is primarily used by businesses. This allows companies to reorganize their debts while continuing their operations. The company develops a plan to repay its creditors over time and may negotiate with them to modify the terms of the debt. This type of bankruptcy is often utilized by larger corporations seeking to restructure and remain in business. This may also be an option if part of your debt includes a business.

It is important to note that bankruptcy has significant consequences, including damage to one's credit score and the potential loss of assets. The specifics of bankruptcy laws and proceedings vary by jurisdiction, so it is highly advisable to consult with a bankruptcy attorney or legal professional to understand the implications and navigate the process effectively.

Note: Some of our country's most outstanding and wealthiest leaders have used bankruptcy multiple times in business and seem to have recovered well.

Chapter 10 - Types of Debt

Common Debt

- **Credit card debt** - debt accumulated through the use of credit cards typically carrying High-interest rates
- **Personal loans** - loans obtained from banks and credit unions or online lenders for personal use, often with fixed repayment terms and interest rates.
- **Student loans** - students take on debt to finance their education. These loans can be either federal government backed or private.
- **Mortgage loans** - loans taken to purchase real estate, usually with an extended repayment. The property itself secures these loans.
- **Auto loans** are used to purchase vehicles with the vehicle as collateral.
- **Home equity loans** - loans secured by the equity in a person's home, allowing homeowners to borrow against the value of their property.
- **Payday loans** are short-term loans with high-interest rates, typically repaid on the borrower's next payday.
- **Business loans** - loans businesses obtain to finance operations expansions or specific projects.
- **Medical debt** - debt accumulated for medical expenses, including hospital bills, treatments, or surgeries.
- **Tax debt** - debt owed to the government due to unpaid taxes or underpayment.
- **Overdraft debt** - debt incurred when a person spends more money than they have available in their Bank account, resulting in negative balances and associated fees.
- **Lines of Credit** - revolving credit lines provided by financial institutions, allowing borrowers to access funds up to a predetermined limit.
- **Store credit** - debt accumulated through financing options provided by retail stores allowing customers to make purchases and pay over time.
- **Consolidation loans** - loans taken to pay off multiple existing debts, combining them into a single loan with one monthly payment.
- **Installment loans** are loans repaid over a set period with fixed monthly payments, such as furniture or appliance loans.
- **Utility Bill Debt** – Unpaid bills for utilities such as electric, water, or gas.
- **Child support debt** – debt owed for unpaid child support obligations.
- **Alimony debt** – debt resulting from unpaid alimony or spousal support payments.
- **Rent-to-own debt** – debt incurred when leasing and gradually paying for items, such as furniture or appliances, with the option to own them eventually.
- **Collection agency debt** – debt sold to a collection agency after being delinquent or unpaid for some time.

It is important to note that each type of debt may have different terms, interest rates, and repayment schedules.

Uncommon Debt

There are some uncommon types of debt that you may not encounter.

- **Peer-to-Peer (P2P) lending** - this type of debt involves barring money from individuals through online platforms that connect borrowers with lenders directly. P2P lending cuts out traditional financial institutions allowing borrowers to access funds from Individual investors.
- **Car title loans** - using a vehicle's title as collateral for short-term, high-interest loans. If the borrower fails to repay the loan, the lender can repossess the car.
- **Gambling debt** - this type of debt arises when individuals borrow money to fund their gambling activities, often resulting in significant financial difficulties and addiction-related issues.
- **Legal settlement debt** - if an individual loses a lawsuit or settles a legal case, they may be required to pay a substantial sum over time. This debt may result from personal injury claims, civil lawsuits, or other legal matters.
- **Court Ordered judgments** – debt resulting from legal judgments, including fines, settlements, or awarded damages.
- **Cryptocurrency debt** - with the growing popularity of cryptocurrencies, some individuals may accrue debt by trading or investing in digital currencies and experience losses due to market volatility.
- **Art loans** - some individuals may take out loans against valuable artwork they own. The artwork secures these loans and is typically offered by specialized lenders or art financing companies.
- **Vacation loans** - some lenders offer loans specifically designed for financing vacations or travel. Borrowers can use the funds to cover flights, accommodations, and activities.
- **Esports loans** - as professional esports and gaming continue to grow, players may take out loans to finance their training, equipment purchases, or participation in esports tournaments.
- **Royalty advances** – musicians, authors, or other creators with future royalty income streams may opt to receive an advance on their future earnings in exchange for a percentage of those royalties.
- **Inheritance advances** - some companies are for loans or advances to individuals entitled to inheritance but need immediate access to the funds before the estate is settled.

It is important to note that while these types of debts are less common, they can still have profound implications for individuals' financial well-being. It's always advisable to exercise caution and make informed decisions when considering taking on any form of debt.

Chapter 11 - List of Expenses

Remember that this list is not exhaustive, and other expenses may be specific to your situation. It's essential to track and budget for all your costs to manage your finances effectively.

Housing Expenses
- rent or mortgage payments
- property taxes
- homeowners' or renters' insurance
- utilities, electricity, water, gas, etc.
- Maintenance and repairs

Transportation Expenses
- vehicle loan or lease payments
- fuel or public transportation costs
- vehicle insurance
- maintenance and repairs
- parking fees
- driver's license fees
- traffic and ticket violation fees

Food Expenses
- Groceries
- dining out or ordering takeout
- snacks and beverages

Personal Care Expenses
- toiletries
- haircuts or salon services
- makeup and skin care products

Healthcare Expenses
- health insurance premiums
- doctor visit co-pays and prescriptions
- dental and vision care
- medical supplies or equipment

Education Expenses
- tuition fees
- books and supplies
- student loans or scholarships
- education programs or courses
- other college expenses

Debt Payments
- credit card payments
- loan repayments (personal and student, etc.)
- interest payments

Entertainment Expenses
- movie tickets or streaming services
- internet, cable services
- concert or live performances
- hobbies or recreational activities
- vacations or travel expenses

Insurance Premiums
- life insurance
- disability insurance
- long-term care insurance
- auto insurance
- burial insurance

Child Care Expenses
- daycare or babysitting costs
- school tuition fees
- extracurricular activities

Pets
- food and water
- grooming services
- vet care
- toys and bedding
- pet daycare or pet-sitting service

Taxes
- income taxes
- property taxes
- sales taxes

Charitable Donations
- contributions to nonprofit organizations
- religious donations

Subscriptions and Memberships
- magazine or newspaper subscriptions
- gym or club memberships
- online streaming services
- car maintenance plans
- home repair plans
- software subscriptions

Personal Expenses Finance
- financial advisor fees
- bank fees
- investment fees
- software or tools for budgeting or tracking expenses

Miscellaneous Expenses
- clothing and accessories
- home furnishings
- gifts and donations

Chapter 12 - Simple Everyday Money-Savings Tips

It is essential to understand that cutting costs and saving money are key factors. Remember that some may require purchases for you to make, so make sure to account for those costs in your budget. These initial investments will yield long-term savings. Here are some money-saving ideas:

How to Save on Finances and Shopping

Evaluate your bank accounts – Whether you have a checking, savings, money markets, etc. Always make sure your bank is not charging you overdraft fees, monthly maintenance fees, etc. Most online banks no longer charge those annoying fees even when you are at fault. Consider this an option if your current bank charges fees or refuses to remove them when asked.

Buy in bulk – Consider purchasing nonperishable items in bulk. Sometimes these items are cheaper, mainly if you use them regularly and they have a long shelf life.

Cashback programs – Take advantage of cashback programs when you shop online. These sites will give you cash back on many places that you may shop. When your budget allows and you make an online purchase, using a cashback site will give you money back after a while in the form of a check or direct deposit. Browse online for cashback sites and sign up.

Save Money For Personal and Medical Care

Personal pampering – If you occasionally spoil yourself with a manicure, pedicure, haircut, or message consider attending a beauty school and allowing the students to perform the services. It is substantially cheaper and, in some cases, free. The students will do an even better job as they are trying to impress their teachers.

Medication/Prescription – Always ask your doctor for samples. Use a drug comparison app to find the cheapest source for filling medications. Request a generic version over the brand name. If the brand name is the only option, log in to the manufacturer's site to see if they have coupons or membership to purchase the medication at a fixed price.

How to Save Money In Your Home

Remove the landline – Do you need the added cost of the landline? Consider porting the number over to your cell phone and save money. Most activities (family, friends, banking, employer, etc.) now require a cell phone number, not a landline.

Save on cable, TV, and Cell Phones – Cable companies can charge up to $200+ per month on some basic TV and internet. How many of those channels do you watch? Consider shopping for internet costs; most cell phone carriers offer home internet service that can be bundled with your cell phone, plus offer a free streaming service. Consider streaming services that are free or have a subscription for less than $10.00/month. With the purchase of some smart TV brands, they come prebuilt with their free streaming channels. For the diamonds stuck in the rough kind of programs, check out www.kicklinetv.com where it's free to watch.

Plant some trees – Planting deciduous trees are great for energy savings because they provide shade during the summer months and allow sunlight to reach your home during the winter when they lose their leaves. (Ex. oak, maple, birch, and ash trees) Consider also evergreen trees as they provide year-round shade and windbreaks, reducing heat loss in the winter. (Ex. pine, spruce, cedar, and cypress)

Do household chores at night – Utility companies have rates for when you use your utility. Find out the peak and off-peak hours and the rates. Use the off-peak hours to use your dishwasher, washer, dryer and even run the vacuum. You can even have your utility company run an audit free of charge, and they can suggest ways to cut costs. Sometimes, they will even provide you with free energy savings devices.

Use a programmable thermostat – Automatically changing the temperature in your home to optimize when you are home, out, or sleeping can add up. In the summer, each degree the thermostat is up can mean a 2-5% savings on your electric bill. In the winter, each degree lower can have similar savings. Overall give yourself up to a 30% savings in your utility bills.

Cold water washing – most laundry detergents are now advanced enough to clean in hot and cold water. Skipping the added heat for hot water and doing your laundry in cold water will help you save about $.50/load.

Reduce the temperature on your water heater – Save about 5% for each 10-degree reduction in temperature. Use a setting of 120 degrees or less to get the maximum savings.

Make your own cleaning supplies – browse online for formulas to make your cleaning supplies out of non-toxic ingredients. Most are items you may already have in your home. What a way to save money and keep your home clean.

Home Maintenance – Whether changing the filters once a month on your HVAC unit, vacuuming coils behind your fridge, cleaning the vents from your dryers, etc. Pay attention to the home maintenance of your appliances and cleaning routines. Maintenance will save you money on repair and replacement costs.

How to Save Money with Your Car

Save money on car insurance – Shop around. If situations have changed and your children are in college over 100 miles away, good student discounts, tell your insurance company to see if they have discounts that you qualify for.

Carpooling/Public Transit – If you drive to work and have coworkers near you, try carpooling once a week. You will save money and wear and tear on your vehicle. Use another day of the week to commute. The cost on that day will be less than gas, mileage, and sometimes, tolls.

Car maintenance – Some people never do maintenance on their vehicle until there is a problem. With proper care, you prolong or avoid those costly repair problems from happening. Oil changes, adequate inflation of tires, etc., can also save you gas consumption on gas-operated vehicles. Please keep track of your vehicle's maintenance suggestions and get them done. Saving money on repairs through maintenance is critical.

Save Money on Entertainment and Family Fun

Streaming services share – Share an account with a family member or friend. Most streaming services will give you up to 2-3 simultaneous access accounts per subscription.

Visit your local library – Your local library has tons of books, videos, and music that you can borrow instead of rent or purchase. Now the library has connections with multiple libraries throughout the country, so if they don't have exactly what you are looking for, they can have it shipped in for you at no cost.

Visit family venues – Research museums, zoos, national parks, etc., and find their free admission days. Consider matinees when it comes time to take in a movie. All theatres offer discounted prices on their first showing of the day or any time before the evening showing, especially on the weekends.

Happy Hour at home – Purchase your favorite hooch or beer by the case. Most on-premise establishments charge 3x of their wholesale costs for the alcohol they purchase (mixed drinks included). A glass of wine will cost you what they paid wholesale for the entire bottle. With off-premise establishments, the markup is only 1/3 of their cost. Much cheaper to drink at home. If you must make a trip to your favorite libation spot, go during their happy hour, where the drinks, appetizers, and lite bites are discounted, or there is a 2-for-1 offer.

Homemade gift giving – When it comes to giving gifts, tap into your creative side and make homemade gifts and cards. This is how sites like Etsy are so popular. It's mostly creative people tapping into their creative side and making homemade items to sell. Paying $6.00 for a greeting card when you can make one just as meaningful is a no-brainer.

Potluck parties – Next time you want to throw a social gathering, make it a potluck party in your online invites. When your guests RSVP, also have them identify what they are bringing. You can even have suggested items they can choose to get.

Chapter 13 - Workbook Samples

Debt Building Worksheet (Sample)

Debt Building Worksheet		
Monthly	**Quarterly**	**Annually**
Credit Cards (8)	Tax (1)	Tax (2)
Personal Loans (1)		
Car Loans (2)		
Mortgage (1)		
Medical (1)		
Store Credit (4)		
Student Loans (4)		
Utility (2)		

Explanation: These are considered to be "Fixed" expenses. They are the same amount each month, quarter, or annually when they are paid.

The above is a sample of a Debt Build for a person who has:

Monthly Payments of:

8 different credit cards

1 Personal Loan

2 car loans

1 mortgage

1 Medical bill

4 different store credit cards

4 different student loans

2 utility pay-off bills – Utility bill arrears that are being paid off. This should not be mistaken for the utility bill expense.

Quarterly Payment of

1 Tax debt

Annual Payment of

1 Tax debt

Fixed Expense Worksheet (Sample)

Fixed Expense Worksheet							
Debt	**Due Date**	**Minimum Amount Due**	**Payoff Balance**	**10% Payoff Balance**	**25% Payoff Balance**	**50% Payoff Balance**	**Interest Rate**
Savings	1st	$300.00	$10,000.00	$1,000.00	$2,500.00	$5,000.00	0.00%
Mortgage	1st	$3500.00	$184,375	$18437.50	$46,093.75	$92,187.50	6.99%
Credit Card 1	2nd	$175.00	$5005.77	$500.58	$1251.44	$2502.89	29.99%
Credit Card 2	3rd	$156.00	$4463.54	$446.35	$1,115.89	$2,231.77	19.99%
Credit Card 3	4th	$150.00	$10,000.00	$1,000.00	$2,500.00	$5,000.00	24.99%
Credit Card 4	5th	$100.00	$8500.00	$850.00	$2,125.00	$4,250.00	16.00%
Credit Card 5	6th	$225.00	$16,850.33	$1,685,03	$4.212.58	$8,425.17	12.00%
Credit Card 6	7th	$25.00	$525.00	$52.50	$131.25	$262.50	29.00%
Credit Card 7	8th	$30.00	$1300.00	$130.00	$325.00	$650.00	27.99%
Credit Card 8	9th	$36.00	$886.41	$88.64	$221.60	$443.21	22.24%
Personal Loans	10th	$225.00	$6670.45	$667.05	$1,667.61	$3,335.23	28.98%
Car Loans 1	11th	$586.00	$27,278.37	$2,727.84	$6,819.59	$13,639.19	11.5%
Car Loans 2	14th	$400.00	$8,779.32	$877.93	$2194.83	$4,389.66	10.99%
Medical	15th	$67.00	$2,304.02	$230.40	$576.01	$1,152.01	0.00%
Store Credit 1	16th	$29.00	$995.00	$99.50	$248.75	$497.50	19.99%
Store Credit 2	17th	$35.00	$,1500.00	$150.00	$375.00	$750.00	18.75%
Store Credit 3	18th	$39.00	$2,200.00	$220.00	$550.00	$1,100.00	18.00%
Store Credit 4	19th	$30.00	$379.00	$37.90	$94.75	$189.50	22.00%
Student Loans 1	20th	$120.00	$3,474.68	$347.47	$868.67	$1,737.34	14.38%
Student Loans 2	21st	$150.00	$5,000.00	$500.00	$1,250.00	$2,500.00	14.00%
Student Loans 3	22nd	$50.00	$12,000.00	$1,200.00	$3,000.00	$6,000.00	14.00%
Student Loans 4	23rd	$600.00	$75,000.00	$7,500.00	$18,750.00	$37,500.00	14.00%
Utility 1	24th	$100.00	$1,000.00	$100.00	$150.00	$500.00	0.00%
Utility 2	25th	$50.00	$500.00	$50.00	$75.00	$250.00	0.00%
Tax	26th	$1,000	$17,000	$1,700.00	$4,250.00	$8,500.00	0.00%
Total		$7,878.00	$395,986.89	$39,601.66	$94,638.93	$197,993.47	

As mentioned before, paying yourself first will force you to look at savings as a priority. Consider a dollar amount you want to save for a purpose and place that at the beginning of your fixed expense. This way, you will always have it in your budget to pay. You will learn about allocating for other savings in the budget sheet.

Explanation: Now that we identified all our debt from the debt building worksheet, here is where we break down the details for each debt that we need for our budget. The sample above is a partial account of all debt, as you would also include your fixed expenses. However, this is used for example purposes.

It is important to have this complete breakdown as you will decide what you will pay on each debt and apply the blueprint to pay these off ultimately.

Using the Debt Avalanche from the blueprint, Credit Card 1 should be your target as it has an interest rate of 29.99%, the highest of all the debts listed above. Follow closely Credit Card 6, with a 29% interest rate.

Using the Debt Snowball from the blueprint, Store Credit Card 4 should be your target as it is the lowest debt that could be paid off in full quicker than all the others. Follow closely by Utility 2 at $500.

Note: Credit Card 6 can apply both the Debt Snowball and Debt Avalanche as it has the highest interest rate and one of the lowest balances. Making this a priority to pay this off is a win-win!

Creating the expense worksheet in a spreadsheet is optimal. The ease of being able to sort by interest rates, due dates, final balances, or even the percentages of the payoff balances will give you a view of what can be paid based on your budget allowances. For instance, you came into some extra cash and want to apply it to your debt. Sorting your debt by any column header will allow you to identify where to use the extra money. For example, you won a cash prize of $2,000.00, and you want to apply it to pay down your debt. What would be some of your options?

- Make a 10% payoff to Credit Card 3 of $1,000 and your personal loan for $667.03. You would have some left over to pay 10% off a few store cards.
- You could apply the entire $2,000 to your highest debt and use the Debt Avalanche method.
- Make an additional or higher payment to a bunch of your "low hanging fruit" cards to get them paid off, or bring the amount lower so you can pay them off by the next month's payment or shortly after that.

These are just a few scenarios, with no right or wrong answer. It is what is best that you will feel comfortable about getting closer to your pay-off goals. You can review your budget to make the final determination. Your budget will be your guide and plan on what to do next.

Variable Expense Worksheet (Sample)

Variable Expense Worksheet	
Variable Expense Category	**Average Monthly Amount**
Groceries	$500.00
Personal Care	$200.00
Clothing	$50.00
Health	$100.00
Dining Out	$300.00
Entertainment	$250.00
Car Maintenance	$150.00
	$
	$
	$
	$
	$
	$
	$
Total	**$1550.00**

Explanation – In the variable expense list, you must consider all your variable expenses, from personal care to groceries, to entertainment. Think about all that you have and will spend each month. Is it a holiday month? Does your car(s) need maintenance this month? Annual DMV or Driver's license renewal due? This is what you have to think about each month and during the month to update your variable expenses.

Budget Worksheet Sample

Monthly Budget – XX/XXXX (Month/Year)

Monthly Income	
Income Source 1	$6000.00
Income Source 2	$2000.00
Bonus Income	$750.00
Total	$8750.00

Monthly Budget Total	
Total Income	$8750.00
(Minus)	
Total Expenses	$8,750.00
Final Budget	**$0.00**

Fixed Expenses		
Expense	**Budgeted**	**Spent**
Mortgage	$3500.00	$3500.00
Car Loans 1	$586.00	$586.00
Car Loans 2	$400.00	$400.00
Internet	$59.00	$59.00
Cell Phone	$150.00	$150.00
Auto Insurance	$100.00	$100.00
Health Insurance	$50.00	$50.00
Student Loans 1	$120.00	$120.00
Student Loans 2	$150.00	$150.00
Student Loans 3	$50.00	$50.00
Student Loans 4	$600.00	$600.00
Total	$5765.00	$5765.00

Variable Expenses		
Expense	**Budgeted**	**Spent**
Groceries	$500.00	$250.00
Personal Care	$200.00	$75.00
Clothing	$50.00	$25.00
Health	$100.00	$50.00
Dining Out	$300.00	$100.00
Entertainment	$250.00	$100.00
Hobby	$25.00	$25.00
Fuel	$150.00	$150.00
Gas	$100.00	$75.00
Electric	$100.00	$100.00
Water	$25.00	$25.00
	$	$
Total	$1800.00	$975.00

Debt		
Debt	**Budgeted**	**Spent**
Credit Card 1	$175.00	$175.00
Credit Card 2	$156.00	$156.00
Credit Card 3	$150.00	$150.00
Credit Card 4	$100.00	$100.00
Credit Card 5	$225.00	$225.00
Credit Card 6	$25.00	$25.00
Credit Card 7	$30.00	$30.00
Credit Card 8	$36.00	$36.00
Personal Loans	$225.00	$225.00
Utility 1	$100.00	$100.00
Utility 2	$50.00	$50.00
Medical	$67.00	$67.00
Store Credit 1	$29.00	$29.00
Store Credit 2	$35.00	$35.00
Store Credit 3	$39.00	$39.00
Store Credit 4	$30.00	$30.00
Total	**$1472.00**	**$1472.00**

Savings		
	Budgeted	Spent
Emergency Fund	$100.00	$100.00
Retirement	$250.00	$250.00
Savings	$100.00	$125.00
Giving	$50.00	$63.00
Total	$500.00	$538.00

Explanation:

Your Monthly Income – Ensure you include all incomes and any unexpected funds received as bonus money. Add up all your paychecks, which you must write down on your monthly budget. If you have varied income, put down the least amount you are expected to earn, and you can constantly adjust.

List all your Bills/Expenses – Use the fixed expense worksheet to list your recurring fixed expenses. Make sure to write these bills on your "Fixed Expenses". Identify and list all your variable expenses under your budget's "Variable Expenses" section. Use the blank lines in the Variable Expense section to personalize those expenses.

Subtract your Total Income from your Expenses. ***This should always equal zero***. The main goal is to develop a zero-based budget. Every dollar of income is being budgeted. If you have a positive number, allocate your extra money towards your own money goals or additional savings. You can save for a new car or grow a more extensive emergency savings account. If you come up with a negative number, look at your variable expenses and see where you can cut back. You may be comfortable only spending $150/month on entertainment instead of $250/mo. Adjust your variable expenses until you end up with $0.00

Update Frequently – Keep track of all your spending so you narrow down and perfect your variable expense values on your budget. Consider this a weekly review to stay on budget and not lose track of your financial goals.

Workbooks

Debt Building Worksheet

Debt Building Worksheet		
Monthly	**Quarterly**	**Annually**

Debt Building Worksheet		
Monthly	**Quarterly**	**Annually**

Debt Building Worksheet		
Monthly	**Quarterly**	**Annually**

Debt Building Worksheet		
Monthly	**Quarterly**	**Annually**

Debt Building Worksheet		
Monthly	**Quarterly**	**Annually**

Debt Building Worksheet		
Monthly	**Quarterly**	**Annually**

Debt Building Worksheet		
Monthly	**Quarterly**	**Annually**

Debt Building Worksheet		
Monthly	**Quarterly**	**Annually**

Debt Building Worksheet		
Monthly	**Quarterly**	**Annually**

Debt Building Worksheet		
Monthly	**Quarterly**	**Annually**

Debt Building Worksheet		
Monthly	**Quarterly**	**Annually**

Debt Building Worksheet		
Monthly	**Quarterly**	**Annually**

Debt Building Worksheet		
Monthly	**Quarterly**	**Annually**

Debt Building Worksheet		
Monthly	**Quarterly**	**Annually**

Debt Building Worksheet		
Monthly	**Quarterly**	**Annually**

Debt Building Worksheet		
Monthly	**Quarterly**	**Annually**

Debt Building Worksheet		
Monthly	**Quarterly**	**Annually**

Debt Building Worksheet		
Monthly	**Quarterly**	**Annually**

Fixed Expense Worksheet

Fixed Expense Worksheet							
Debt	**Due Date**	**Minimum Amount Due**	**Payoff Balance**	**10% Payoff Balance**	**25% Payoff Balance**	**50% Payoff Balance**	**Interest Rate**
Total							

Fixed Expense Worksheet

Debt	Due Date	Minimum Amount Due	Payoff Balance	10% Payoff Balance	25% Payoff Balance	50% Payoff Balance	Interest Rate
Total							

Fixed Expense Worksheet							
Debt	**Due Date**	**Minimum Amount Due**	**Payoff Balance**	**10% Payoff Balance**	**25% Payoff Balance**	**50% Payoff Balance**	**Interest Rate**
Total							

Fixed Expense Worksheet

Debt	Due Date	Minimum Amount Due	Payoff Balance	10% Payoff Balance	25% Payoff Balance	50% Payoff Balance	Interest Rate
Total							

Fixed Expense Worksheet

Debt	Due Date	Minimum Amount Due	Payoff Balance	10% Payoff Balance	25% Payoff Balance	50% Payoff Balance	Interest Rate
Total							

Fixed Expense Worksheet							
Debt	**Due Date**	**Minimum Amount Due**	**Payoff Balance**	**10% Payoff Balance**	**25% Payoff Balance**	**50% Payoff Balance**	**Interest Rate**
Total							

Variable Expense Worksheet

Variable Expense Worksheet	
Variable Expense Category	**Average Monthly Amount**
	$
	$
	$
	$
	$
	$
	$
	$
	$
	$
	$
	$
	$
	$
	$
	$
	$
	$
	$
	$
	$
	$
	$
Total	**$**

Variable Expense Worksheet	
Variable Expense Category	**Average Monthly Amount**
	$
	$
	$
	$
	$
	$
	$
	$
	$
	$
	$
	$
	$
	$
	$
	$
	$
	$
	$
	$
	$
	$
	$
Total	**$**

Variable Expense Worksheet	
Variable Expense Category	**Average Monthly Amount**
	$
	$
	$
	$
	$
	$
	$
	$
	$
	$
	$
	$
	$
	$
	$
	$
	$
	$
	$
	$
	$
	$
	$
Total	**$**

Variable Expense Worksheet	
Variable Expense Category	**Average Monthly Amount**
	$
	$
	$
	$
	$
	$
	$
	$
	$
	$
	$
	$
	$
	$
	$
	$
	$
	$
	$
	$
	$
	$
	$
Total	**$**

Variable Expense Worksheet	
Variable Expense Category	**Average Monthly Amount**
	$
	$
	$
	$
	$
	$
	$
	$
	$
	$
	$
	$
	$
	$
	$
	$
	$
	$
	$
	$
	$
	$
	$
Total	**$**

Variable Expense Worksheet	
Variable Expense Category	**Average Monthly Amount**
	$
	$
	$
	$
	$
	$
	$
	$
	$
	$
	$
	$
	$
	$
	$
	$
	$
	$
	$
	$
	$
	$
	$
Total	**$**

Budget Worksheet

Monthly Budget –

Monthly Income	
Income Source 1	$
Income Source 2	$
Bonus Income	$
Total	$

Monthly Budget Total	
Total Income	$
(Minus)	
Total Expenses	$
Final Budget	$

Fixed Expenses		
Expense	Budgeted	Spent
	$	$
	$	$
	$	$
	$	$
	$	$
	$	$
	$	$
	$	$
	$	$
	$	$
	$	$
	$	$
	$	$
	$	$
Total	$	$

Variable Expenses		
Expense	Budgeted	Spent
	$	$
	$	$
	$	$
	$	$
	$	$
	$	$
	$	$
	$	$
	$	$
	$	$
	$	$
	$	$
Total	$	$

Debt		
Debt	Budgeted	Spent
	$	$
	$	$
	$	$
	$	$
	$	$
	$	$
	$	$
	$	$
	$	$
	$	$
	$	$
	$	$
	$	$
	$	$
	$	$
	$	$
	$	$
	$	$
	$	$
	$	$
	$	$
	$	$
Total	$	$

Savings		
	Budgeted	Spent
Emergency Fund	$	$
Retirement	$	$
Savings	$	$
Giving	$	$
Total	$	$

Monthly Budget –

Monthly Income	
Income Source 1	$
Income Source 2	$
Bonus Income	$
Total	$

Monthly Budget Total	
Total Income	$
(Minus)	
Total Expenses	$
Final Budget	$

Fixed Expenses		
Expense	**Budgeted**	**Spent**
	$	$
	$	$
	$	$
	$	$
	$	$
	$	$
	$	$
	$	$
	$	$
	$	$
	$	$
	$	$
	$	$
	$	$
Total	$	$

Debt		
Debt	**Budgeted**	**Spent**
	$	$
	$	$
	$	$
	$	$
	$	$
	$	$
	$	$
	$	$
	$	$
	$	$
	$	$
	$	$
	$	$
	$	$
	$	$
	$	$
	$	$
	$	$
	$	$
	$	$
	$	$
	$	$
Total	$	$

Variable Expenses		
Expense	**Budgeted**	**Spent**
	$	$
	$	$
	$	$
	$	$
	$	$
	$	$
	$	$
	$	$
	$	$
	$	$
	$	$
	$	$
Total	$	$

Savings		
	Budgeted	Spent
Emergency Fund	$	$
Retirement	$	$
Savings	$	$
Giving	$	$
Total	$	$

Monthly Budget –

Monthly Income	
Income Source 1	$
Income Source 2	$
Bonus Income	$
Total	$

Monthly Budget Total	
Total Income	$
(Minus)	
Total Expenses	$
Final Budget	$

Fixed Expenses		
Expense	**Budgeted**	**Spent**
	$	$
	$	$
	$	$
	$	$
	$	$
	$	$
	$	$
	$	$
	$	$
	$	$
	$	$
	$	$
	$	$
	$	$
Total	$	$

Variable Expenses		
Expense	**Budgeted**	**Spent**
	$	$
	$	$
	$	$
	$	$
	$	$
	$	$
	$	$
	$	$
	$	$
	$	$
	$	$
	$	$
Total	$	$

Debt		
Debt	**Budgeted**	**Spent**
	$	$
	$	$
	$	$
	$	$
	$	$
	$	$
	$	$
	$	$
	$	$
	$	$
	$	$
	$	$
	$	$
	$	$
	$	$
	$	$
	$	$
	$	$
	$	$
	$	$
	$	$
	$	$
Total	$	$

Savings		
	Budgeted	Spent
Emergency Fund	$	$
Retirement	$	$
Savings	$	$
Giving	$	$
Total	$	$

Monthly Budget –

Monthly Income	
Income Source 1	$
Income Source 2	$
Bonus Income	$
Total	$

Monthly Budget Total	
Total Income	$
(Minus)	
Total Expenses	$
Final Budget	$

Fixed Expenses		
Expense	**Budgeted**	**Spent**
	$	$
	$	$
	$	$
	$	$
	$	$
	$	$
	$	$
	$	$
	$	$
	$	$
	$	$
	$	$
	$	$
	$	$
Total	$	$

Variable Expenses		
Expense	**Budgeted**	**Spent**
	$	$
	$	$
	$	$
	$	$
	$	$
	$	$
	$	$
	$	$
	$	$
	$	$
	$	$
	$	$
Total	$	$

Debt		
Debt	**Budgeted**	**Spent**
	$	$
	$	$
	$	$
	$	$
	$	$
	$	$
	$	$
	$	$
	$	$
	$	$
	$	$
	$	$
	$	$
	$	$
	$	$
	$	$
	$	$
	$	$
	$	$
	$	$
	$	$
	$	$
Total	$	$

Savings		
	Budgeted	Spent
Emergency Fund	$	$
Retirement	$	$
Savings	$	$
Giving	$	$
Total	$	$

Monthly Budget –

Monthly Income	
Income Source 1	$
Income Source 2	$
Bonus Income	$
Total	$

Monthly Budget Total	
Total Income	$
(Minus)	
Total Expenses	$
Final Budget	$

Fixed Expenses		
Expense	**Budgeted**	**Spent**
	$	$
	$	$
	$	$
	$	$
	$	$
	$	$
	$	$
	$	$
	$	$
	$	$
	$	$
	$	$
	$	$
	$	$
Total	$	$

Variable Expenses		
Expense	**Budgeted**	**Spent**
	$	$
	$	$
	$	$
	$	$
	$	$
	$	$
	$	$
	$	$
	$	$
	$	$
	$	$
	$	$
Total	$	$

Debt		
Debt	**Budgeted**	**Spent**
	$	$
	$	$
	$	$
	$	$
	$	$
	$	$
	$	$
	$	$
	$	$
	$	$
	$	$
	$	$
	$	$
	$	$
	$	$
	$	$
	$	$
	$	$
	$	$
	$	$
	$	$
	$	$
Total	$	$

Savings		
	Budgeted	Spent
Emergency Fund	$	$
Retirement	$	$
Savings	$	$
Giving	$	$
Total	$	$

Monthly Budget –

Monthly Income	
Income Source 1	$
Income Source 2	$
Bonus Income	$
Total	$

Monthly Budget Total	
Total Income	$
(Minus)	
Total Expenses	$
Final Budget	$

Fixed Expenses		
Expense	**Budgeted**	**Spent**
	$	$
	$	$
	$	$
	$	$
	$	$
	$	$
	$	$
	$	$
	$	$
	$	$
	$	$
	$	$
	$	$
	$	$
Total	$	$

Variable Expenses		
Expense	**Budgeted**	**Spent**
	$	$
	$	$
	$	$
	$	$
	$	$
	$	$
	$	$
	$	$
	$	$
	$	$
	$	$
	$	$
Total	$	$

Debt		
Debt	**Budgeted**	**Spent**
	$	$
	$	$
	$	$
	$	$
	$	$
	$	$
	$	$
	$	$
	$	$
	$	$
	$	$
	$	$
	$	$
	$	$
	$	$
	$	$
	$	$
	$	$
	$	$
	$	$
	$	$
	$	$
Total	$	$

Savings		
	Budgeted	Spent
Emergency Fund	$	$
Retirement	$	$
Savings	$	$
Giving	$	$
Total	$	$

Conclusion

I emphasize the importance of clearly understanding your financial situation and setting achievable goals. By implementing the proven strategies outlined in this book, you can take proactive steps toward eliminating debt and free yourself from the burdensome cycle of interest payments. Furthermore, you don't just focus on debt repayment; it also emphasizes the significance of saving and building a solid financial foundation for the future.

This book provides practical advice on creating and maintaining a budget, maximizing income, and making intelligent financial choices to ensure long-term financial stability. By combining the principles of debt reduction and savings growth, you can create a solid financial framework that promotes both short-term relief and long-term prosperity. The strategies presented are designed to empower you to take control of your economic destinies, break free from the shackles of debt, and embark on a path toward your financial goals. Let this valuable resource equip you with the knowledge and tools necessary to conquer debt and cultivate a healthy financial future. Let it serve as a roadmap, guiding you through each step of the journey toward debt freedom. With commitment, discipline, patience, and guidance in this book, you can transform your financial life and experience the peace of mind that comes with being debt-free.

NOTES

NOTES

NOTES

NOTES

NOTES

NOTES

NOTES

NOTES

NOTES

Special Thanks

Special thanks to the following who were patient with me during this process:
Christian, Kay, Stephanie, Waffles, Mason, Mittens, Mr. Milo Brown, Mystique, Mink, and Maui.

A Big Thank You to www.SFLiteraryPress.com and their donation to www.CampMaranacookArts.org
Gratitude to www.LibWalt.com for the great launching gadgets.

About the Author

Victoria Gunn has made a significant impact in the fields of finance, travel, writing, and entrepreneurial strategies. With her extensive knowledge and expertise, she has established herself as a financial expert, world traveler, published author, and guru on entrepreneurial strategy.

With a background and degree in finance, Victoria has spent years honing her skills and gaining valuable experience in the industry. She has an in-depth understanding of practical financial strategies, consumer and business credit, and economic trends, allowing her to provide expert advice and guidance to individuals and businesses. Her keen insights and ability to analyze complex financial data have earned her a reputation as a trusted authority in the field.

Victoria's passion for exploring new cultures and experiencing diverse perspectives has taken her on countless adventures worldwide. She has traveled to numerous countries, immersing herself in different traditions, languages, and customs. Her global travels have broadened her horizons and provided her with unique insights into the global economy and business practices.

As a published author, Victoria has shared her expertise and experiences through her acclaimed books. Her writings cover various topics, including personal finance, entrepreneurship, children's books, and fiction writings. Her ability to convey complex concepts clearly and engagingly has made her books popular among readers looking for practical advice and inspiration.

Victoria's entrepreneurial acumen sets her apart as a guru in the field. She deeply understands the challenges and opportunities that arise in the business world. Her strategic thinking, innovative approach, and ability to identify emerging trends have helped countless aspiring entrepreneurs and established businesses succeed. She has empowered individuals to transform their ideas into thriving enterprises through her mentorship, workshops, and consulting services.

With her diverse talents and accomplishments, Victoria Gunn inspires and motivates others to achieve financial independence, explore the world, unleash their creativity, and build successful businesses. Her dedication to helping others achieve their goals has made her a highly sought-after advisor, speaker, and influencer.

Victoria is a true animal lover and has several rescue pets.

Made in the USA
Monee, IL
02 November 2026

67382290R00044